I0052998

# *Business* SUCCESS STRATEGIES *for* WOMEN ON THE RISE

*Editor*
**Yvette Salomon**

# MARSHA GUERRIER

*Women on the Rise NY, Inc. Publishing*
*Valley Stream, NY*

Copyright © 2018 by Women on the Rise NY, Inc.

All rights reserved. This book or any portion thereof may not be reproduced or used in any manner whatsoever without the express written permission of the publisher except for the use of brief quotations in a book review.

Printed and bound in the United States of America

First Printing October 2018

ISBN 978 - 0 - 9991297 - 6 - 0
Library of Congress Control Number: 2018910380

Women on the Rise NY, Inc. Publishing
P.O. Box 41
Valley Stream, NY 11580

Visit www.womenontheriseny.com

# Dedication

This book is dedicated to all the Women on the Rise working hard to make an impact in the lives of their families and communities. We thank our friends, families and communities for their continued support and love as we pursue our goals and dreams.

# Book Reviews

"The life-altering decisions that matter so much really come from decisions we make every day. They're also the most difficult. Developing the mental toughness and stamina to resist making poor financial decisions is the key to meaningful, long lasting change.

This story will inspire you to gain control of your financial future, chart a path to success and live an enriched life that is free from the burden of financial stress." *-Christopher J. Mahon*

"Get your pen; get your pad take notes, for Tiffany Winfrey of T Smiles Design, Inc. take readers on an endearing journey. Through her personal experience with endings and new beginnings she reaches in and shatters self doubt. *-Diana Whitmore*

"Natasha Nurses' story of perseverance and innovation is one made of the substance of a modern hero. Her ability to dreams into reality allows individuals the gift to live in their own truths. Natasha's wisdom and compassion will live on in infinity in the hearts of those she has inspired, and those she has yet to inspire." *-Terr Cacilia*

The greatest tool Shaquan left me in this book was the unconditional sharing of her failure, only to see her overcome and find the audacity to rise like the mythical phoenix of old. *- Tyrone*

# Contents

# INTRODUCTION
*by*
*Marsha Guerrier*

Let me be honest, in my short time on this earth (that's my story and I'm sticking to it) I've started and ended well over five business. It all started with my ability to craft a resume in high school after taking business courses and working in Corporate America at the age of 16. I used my passions to start businesses like my events planning business, catering services, concierge, home décor and design, I even started washing hair and styling without professional training because I was so passionate about it. The problem was I was passionate about everything and I was just doing what I enjoyed at the time and calling it a business.

My intention was to become an expert in those areas so I can dominate the industry but the truth for me is that it wasn't enough. After changing my major a couple of times I decided the best thing for me was to concentrate on my full time job. But like most entrepreneurs my mind couldn't stop thinking of ways to improve a product or provide a service to someone in need. I needed to get back in the game and this time I knew I was here to stay and I was ready to play!

The only problem was I was afraid to take massive action because I wasn't ready to leave my full time job and I'm still a full time employee in a career I LOVE! I knew this time around I needed more than passion,

I needed a strategy. According to the Small Business Administration 30% of new businesses fail during the first two years of being open, 50% during the first five years and 66% during the first 10. What's great about this statistic is that it means 20% of new businesses succeed during the first two years of being open, 50%during the first five years and 33% during the first 10. How can I be a part of the success ration?

Starting a new business again for me meant that I needed to not only have the vision and passion but I needed a 3 and 5 year plan. First I needed to decide which business I wanted to start and the one thing that kept coming back to me as I was searching for the answers was that I am a connector and an educator. When I looked back at all the companies that I started in the past these two things were the only things that were consistent. With every business, I had the ability to connect my client with the resource they needed and at the same time teach them how to do it for themselves the next time around. Okay I admit that part was crazy because they didn't come back to me because I'm a great teacher. Not a smart money move.

I began with business courses at a state college to spark my interest. It didn't take me long before I decided on a business coaching and consulting business for women.  Based on my past failures I knew the first thing that I needed to succeed was the right mindset about being an entrepreneur. I knew I had to think bigger even while working in a small capacity. Did you get that? In order for me to know what I needed to do today for my business I needed to see realistically what my business could look like in the future. I set out to create my big idea business plan, while I was working full time and taking clients. You see its okay to start the business while you are building your strategy plan; it helps you get clarity as you are writing the vision.

Many of you, again like I did years ago, are working your business without proper legal structures to protect you. The first thing to do when training your mindset as an entrepreneur is to actually setup your company with your state and local government offices. The process is SUPER easy and no you don't need to pay someone just to do that. If you are working with a good business coach that person should be able to direct you, hold your hand through the process, while also teaching you and working with you on other areas of your business. Having your company registered makes all the difference in how you make decisions for your business moving forward. You begin to adopt that winning attitude!

The next most important thing I did to get in the proper business mindset was to open my business bank account. You may think to yourself but the business money is my money, yeah we know. Separating your business money from your personal money, even if the money is coming from the same source in the beginning will allow you to better understand what your business expenses are because we know in the beginning there's nothing but expenses. Most importantly, your business account will make it easier comes tax time for your tax preparer to report your expenses and profits! It's not a bad idea to invest in accounting software so you can quickly upload your transactions and create fancy financial reports. There's nothing like a sexy spreadsheet to make you want to grow your business. These reports will give you the motivation to seek additional funding should you need it. Providing these documents to your initial funders like family and friends will show them that you are serious about your business and they will most likely want to invest in YOU!

After crushing your mindset and attitude it's time to start putting together all the pieces in a business plan. I know you're thinking I can't write a business plan but I know that's not true. You no longer have to write the big book version of a business plan, it's okay to start a simplified version. The business plan will allow you to document and know all the areas that will make your business SOAR like organizational structure, branding, marketing and sales. Most companies, even the big ones are constantly reevaluating their business plans so don't think you need to get it right from the beginning. To help you along the way I will include some basic section of a business plan in this book to help you get started.

When I decided to put this book together, my goal was to provide a resource for new and aspiring entrepreneurs. I believe that so many new entrepreneurs or small business owners start a business just like I did, with passion. But as I learned so many years ago, I know that passion alone will not make success. There is no one path to success and for many, success is a never ending search. These incredible inspiring women you'll meet in this book all used their unique circumstances, skill sets and stories to move themselves forward and achieve success on their own terms. They worked within the parameter of what they had and are now sharing it with you. Through their stories, they're going to provide you strategies so you can draw inspiration and gain success.

Finally, I want to encourage you to take the next step in your journey. Its one thing to read a book and get inspired but it's another thing to actually put what you've learned into action. To discover how you can work with me visit www.womenontheriseny.comor join the Women on the Rise Network at www.womenontherisenetwork.com to network and share your story with other entrepreneurs just like you.

*Marsha Guerrier*

# Chapter 1

## Tiffany Winfrey

## From New to Expert Within A year
A 12-month strategy from launch to business success

I walked this earth for four years with the dream of being a business owner but, yet too afraid to take a leap. A dream that I felt was impossible to achieve. A dream that I thought was not good enough to pursue. My journey started off on a sad note. I took the death of a best friend to help me put the four years behind me and go for what I truly felt in my gut I should have started a long time ago. Do not let the death of someone close to you be your starting ground.

Often known as the quiet friend, I lacked confidence and didn't know the value in my gifts. When it came to changing, I didn't change. When it came to speaking about what I could do, I stuttered. The lack of confidence and not knowing your worth will set you back from being successful every day that you allow it to. Mine lasted four years. How long has yours been?

Allow me to introduce myself; I'm Tiffany Winfrey, CEO, owner and operator of T. Smiles Design, Inc. a small graphic design studio that provides clean, sleek strategic designs to Entrepreneurs, empowering them to declare their value and their mission through their visuals. I launched my business January 4, 2017, on my 32nd birthday and as I write this chapter, today marks 1 year, 6 months, 1 week and 2 days since I've been in business. Since then I've already doubled my revenue, quit my secure, cushioning Corporate job, and am looking to hire an assistant in the next 30 days. But, I was the woman who took 4 years and the loss of a friend to realize that life was short. I've created a solid foundation for myself and have learned the yays, nays, ins, and outs of building a successful business for me.

If you're early on within your business journey, or still stuck within the 'figuring it out phase" or you haven't even reached the confidence and that ah-ha moment where you can really do this, then this is the perfect place to be. I will show you how I went from being a newbie Entrepreneur, working a full-time job, taking care of a home with 2 beautiful stepchildren and their father, to quitting my 6am – 230pm Supervisor position, leaving behind my 1-hour commute to work to become a full-time Entrepreneur and I can show you how you can get there too.

# *Change of Mindset*

To be successful in anything you do, you must first wake up with the desire, the mindset, and the belief that you can and deserve to be successful. To do that a morning routine the vital health of our mind is necessary and the key to being successful. Many people start their morning rushing, but how can they have a clear mind if they're rushing? Changing our mindset to think more positive, driven and successful is hard if we're not aligned with like-minded people. Being around people who are not driven for success will not feed your mind. Sadly, it will do the opposite. If you're primarily the giver you will ultimately feel drained, therefore slowing down productivity.

For instance, when I decided I wanted to quit my job and focus on my business full time, not everyone supported the idea. Most believed that working until I retire with a big fat 401k was the best way to live a long and happy life. Mis-aligned! If I allowed myself to give in to those who weren't in agreement with the way I was thinking, I would still be working my job and texting my friends complaining about work.

Your mindset must be focused on business and succeeding; therefore, you must surround yourself around people who are like-minded and driven like you. Write down 4 people you know around you who are driven, business-minded, always talking about and achieving their goals.

1 _____

2 _____

3 _____

4 _____

You should schedule time with these 4 people NOW. There are 4 weeks in a month so maybe set-up a lunch date with each one every week, or a phone call, or even a video chat. Or if they all know one another, have your own mini lunch mastermind group. You want to be around people who feed and uplift you and you should be able to do the same. In order to be successful, you have to be around like-minded folks. The saying "birds of a feather, flock together" was not made up because it sounded nice.

## *Your First Year in Business*

## *Preparing for Your Launch*

Now that you have the mindset, the drive and you know you CAN be successful. How do you get started?

Research! Reflection! And More Research! Don't you hate when you ask a question and people say "did you Google it?" I'll be honest, Google is my best friend. But the kind of research I'm asking you to do, you can't and won't find on Google. The answers to the questions I ask you can and will only be found from within yourself.

Prior to launching your business, you must prepare. A portion of your preparation should be researching who you are and tying that into the mission and vision of your business. I recommend purchasing a journal. You can purchase any journal or notebook from Target, Staples or Wal-Mart. But, because I love to be extra, TJ Maxx and Marshalls are always my go-to spots for journal shopping. You will take this journal and break it down into 3 sections.

1. MY LIFE/JOURNEY AS A BUSINESS OWNER
2. MY BUSINESS PRAISE REPORTS
3. MY BUSINESS GOALS

**SECTION ONE** – This section is your everyday entries to being an entrepreneur. You will write your feelings, things you are going through on a day-to-day basis as a business owner. This is great to go back and review from time to time to see how much you have grown.

**SECTION TWO**- This is your praise report section– *Gratitude attracts growth*. We must first be thankful for blessings within our businesses, be it a new client/customer or a regular client/customer providing a nice tip. This is great to keep track of in order to go back and review when times are emotionally hard for you. It will be your own personal motivation to push through. Any accomplishment within your business is also a part of the praise report, did you go from a DBA to LLC? This should be noted as well.

**SECTION THREE** - Your goals/ideas for expansion. My best ideas come to me when I'm in the shower. I don't know what that is about, it sucks actually. Can you imagine receiving a great idea in the shower can't write it down then have to force yourself to remember it when you get out? A great friend of mine told me that a random idea that pops into our minds are actually from God and it's why we forget them because it's not our own idea. Can you imagine how important that idea must be then? If it's coming directly from God that should give you all the motivation to make sure you're always walking around with your entrepreneurial journal so that you could write them down.

**SECTION FOUR** - As a BONUS, I want you to flip to the very back of your journal, fold the corner of the page (or put a post it on the edge) and write down 5 things you would like to do within your business journey not this year, but within the next 5 years.

Your first entry into section 1 of your Business Journal, should answer these questions.

1. Who am I? What makes me unique?
2. What business do I wish to start and why?

3. If my friends could describe me, what words would they use?
4. When I wake up in the morning, how do I feel? How would I like to feel?

This is what I mean by researching within you and reflecting. Google can't answer those questions for you. In order to be successful in any business you choose, you must first start with inner reflection on why you're doing what you do. This will help start a solid foundation especially during down moments when your confidence is shaken. Sometimes, we don't realize it but our own words to ourselves can uplift us more than the random quotes on Instagram. Dedicating time to write in your business journal will also help you develop a routine and dedication to your business as it grows.

## *Month 1*
### *Launch. Celebrate. Tell Everyone!!*

Have you ever seen those birthday posts on social media where a person posts "It's My Birthday!!" and everyone comments "Happy Birthday!. By the end of the day, that person has over 100 Happy Birthday comments and emojis! That's how your launch should be. No one will know about you if you're quiet. No one.

If we didn't put our birthday on Facebook, how many people do you think would know to tell us "Happy Birthday"? Crickets. Well, maybe our brother, sister, or crazy Uncle Bill down in Alabama. But other than that, who would know? My first month within launching T. Smiles Design, I received 4 new clients. I'll be honest, for me, it was by accident but I'm telling you so you can do it strategically. I launched on my birthday, January 4th, so instead of saying "Hey it's my Birthday!" on Facebook, I said, "Hey I just started my own business!!" And my God it worked! By the end of January, I was already booked out until March. January alone, I made over $600, that was just starting out. Can you imagine how hype I was?!

So, your first month:

1. Tell all your Facebook friends
2. Join 2 Facebook groups that are local to your area
   a.  Introduce yourself, tell them what you do and how excited you are to just be launching your business.
3. Join 2 Facebook Groups that are pertaining to your market – do the same as the step above
4. Have a launch party – If you do have a launch party, make sure you grab everyone's email address, this will be important for starting your email marketing.
5. Write in your Business Journal – "My Business Praise Reports" – your new clients/customers should be noted for this success

## *Months 2-3*

*A little bit of this, a little bit of that.*

I love buffets. Whoever invented buffets was a genius! I love being able to go to a buffet and have a little bit of this and a little bit of that. Buffets give us a chance to try food we may not necessarily order if it was presented on a menu. This is month 2. Doing this and that and figuring out what works. My second month in business, I had a million applications I was using. My best friend Google told me what the best project management tools were, an invoicing system, a scheduling tool, email marketing application, automation tool and so on. I had so much going on, I was always forgetting passwords. I was all over the place. But, honestly, it was good for me to learn. Some people will tell you, figure it out before you do it, to save yourself time and I get it. But when it comes to developing a system for yourself and your business, the best method to learn is by doing "a little bit of this and a little bit of that" Try different invoicing applications and see which one pays you the quickest and is easy for your clients, then stick with it. Visit back your Business journal, and write down what worked and what didn't work for you and your clients and stick with it.

# *Months 4-6*
## *It's my party, I can cry if I want to.*

Well, the first 3 months, are the exciting months, they're the fun months. Fun because we are newly in love with the idea of full time entrepreneurship. It's an exciting time but now is the time to get serious. Goal serious...Life balance serious!

By month 4 of my business, I was feeling a little overwhelmed. My drive home was 2hrs, I had to pick up the kids, cook, help with homework then work in my business. I was waking up 4 am and going to bed by midnight. It was hard. I wanted to be successful so bad but if felt so hard. Often I cried. I would cry, and then ask myself why am I crying when I should be happy? It felt like too much was going on too fast. In order to not go through the emotions that I went through I suggest that you get organized.

Months 1-3 are your celebrating and learning months. Months 4-6 should be getting organized, setting your goals, being honest with yourself about what works and what doesn't. Set a set schedule for you and your family.

Don't go writing down a goal that says "I want to make a million dollars" when you haven't even made your first thousand. Small increments will help you reach your goal quicker and in a less stressful manner. In the 3$^{rd}$ section of your journal, you will write what systems are in place, as well as create checklists of your day-to-day processes.

By now, you should have figured out what processes work for your business and also have at least 3 months worth of journal entries, praises reports, further business ideas, etc written in your journal. If not, where's your journal? Do you even know where it is? Go grab it. It's important.

Monetary goals should be set as well. Review what you made your first 3 months within the business then set a goal of a 15% increase for the next 3 months.

# *Months 7-9*
## *Just say Yes and do it.*

You already have 6 months of experience under your belt. You're pretty much known within your audience and your business has been rocking and rolling. Earlier in the chapter, I instructed that in the back of your journal you write down things you wanted to do within your business later on. Well, surprise! Guess what I want you to do! I want you to go to that list, pick one thing and do it NOW!! What stops us from growing and being successful is FEAR. I remember writing down that I wanted to be a speaker in two years after launching my business. I felt that in order to be a speaker I needed to be in business for TWO YEARS! That's how I saw it should go for myself. That's how much confidence I lacked in myself. When the opportunity presented itself for me to speak at a Women's Conference, because I had previously written down that it should take me two years, I felt I wasn't equipped yet. But, that was all in my head. With some pushing, of course, I went on to speak for the first time only 8 months after launching my business! This leap of faith to saying YES and just doing it has built a confidence within me that I basically didn't plan to have for another two years. Since then I've been contacted to speak at 5 other events!! Fear is so destructive. So for these 3 months, I want you to choose just one thing you wrote down in the back of your journal and just do it. Don't think how, why, when, can I, will I, nope....just do it! *We often open the gates of success by a shear, YES!*

# *Months 10-12*
## *Review. Regroup. Reward.*

By month 10 within my business, I already knew what NOT to do for my next year. One thing I learned was not to just take on work without reviewing my schedule first. As a business owner, you must know to set the boundary for your time. Boundaries are crucial in relationships and business.

The last 3 months within your year should be all about reviewing your business and yourself. Do you feel you have changed? Do you feel your business has changed in the first 3 months? Do you have a better idea of what kind of clients you'd like to work with? You should be using this time to review your Business Journal, read your daily entries, your praise reports as well as your goals. Did you meet your goals? If not, what stopped you?

Begin planning for your next year. By now your processes should be in place, therefore planning your first 3 months of your 2$^{nd}$ year in business should be a breeze. After you've reviewed and regrouped your first year in business. It's time to reward yourself, treat yourself because you pursued something a lot of people have yet to pursue. A lot of people talk about starting a business but only a few actually do. Reward yourself and know that your next year will be an even bigger reward.

# *About Tiffany Winfrey*

Tiffany Winfrey is a Brand Identity Designer, Speaker and CEO of T. Smiles Design, Inc. T. Smiles Design is an identity design studio that uniquely provides key visual elements a business needs to clarify its mission and value to their audience. Currently located in Queens, NY, Tiffany utilizes her design talents and affable nature to deliver valuable creative solutions as well as enriched client relationships.

Originally from Arkansas, Tiffany moved to New York in 1996 and is known today for her kind southern charm. In 2007, Tiffany received her Bachelor's Degree in Computer Programming Information Services. In which, she then on received the ITIL Certification in Service Management. But, through her experience and qualifications, Tiffany always held a passion for creativity. In 2010, Tiffany followed her inner voice and began painting acrylic based portraits in her free time. She then on transitioned her love of creativity from painting to graphic design. With her passion in place and supporters behind her, Tiffany officially launched T. Smiles Design in January 2017.

As an identity strategist, creative innovator and mentor, Tiffany has been helping businesses establish impactful identities as well as understanding the key essentials of branding. September 2017, Tiffany received the New York State Assembly Certificate of Merit for her service in the community and her support to Women on the Rise.

# RISE SIMPLIFIED BUSINESS PLAN

## EXERCISE #1

## MISSION – VISION – OBJECTIVES – TEAM

Company Name: _____

E-mail: _____ Web Site: _____

Please describe:
1. Your vision for the company (the long-term dream in a perfect world).

2. Your mission for the company (what you'll provide to whom and why).

3. The 3 or 4 major objectives for your business that this plan will help you achieve. Make sure they are specific, measurable, realistic & time-bound.

4. The founders, members and responsibilities of your management team (3-5 people critical to day-to-day operations with greatest impact on future success) – Include their background, the position title, person's name, role (e.g., the duties and responsibilities of the position, what functions they will oversee, who they supervise, who they report to, etc.), and why each is on your team (e.g., previous experience, education and successes relevant to this business to inspire confidence)

# Chapter 2

*Shaquan Hoke*

*Finding Myself Beyond A J.O.B*

I have worked for many companies in various sectors since the age of 14. Never would I have imagined that I would one day own my own consulting company and help change thousands of lives. When I finally stepped into the world of entrepreneurship it was the most amazing and surreal feeling. I must admit that in the beginning of my journey I knew I felt that imposter syndrome that I was not a real CEO. I had that tiny voice that said who are you to call yourself a CEO? Who would actually pay to help them? Before I get into all of this let me share my story with you.

My name is Shaquan Hoke and I am the Founder and CEO of Beyond A J.O.B. Inc. This company was birthed in 2014 after several years of me helping others in the nonprofit organizations of which I've worked. I served clients that were veterans, seniors, young adults and those homeless to name a few. One thing that everyone had in common was that no matter the education level, they all needed job readiness assistance. The clients would find me after leaving the programs they were in to ask for further assistance with resume and job readiness coaching. I've even had clients with Master degree who were far more experienced than me to employ my services. Needless to say that I began to realize that the gift I had to connect clients and employers was something that was desperately needed. The population I service is mostly women aged 30-50 who wanted a career change. I offer group and private training for women including women veterans who are reintegrating into civilian culture. Clients of Beyond a J.O.B. go through our personal development assessment to get clarity on which jobs or careers best suit them before beginning training. They obtain hard and soft skills training, supportive services, financial literacy, employment services and retention. Programs are designed to provide valuable professional development including resume building, interviewing skills and workplace attire.

I am married with five children of my own. At first I had four boys then my daughter was born. I am a Humanitarian who believes in God.

It just so happens that I am an Entrepreneur that uses Beyond A J.O.B. Inc as a conduit to elevate women into economic self-sufficiency.

My family is and has always been my inspiration and driving force. I already know what it feels like to hit rock bottom. While I was in my early twenties as a single parent struggling to make ends meet. Being famous was not even on my "to do" list nor was being rich. Each day I knew I had the goal of earning a living, providing for my children and trying to finish college while worshiping the Lord that seemed to have forgotten me or so I thought. I remembered traveling through three boroughs every day to first take my children to the babysitter and second go to work, and third go to school. The baby sitter lived in Brooklyn, school was in Manhattan and work was in New Jersey. I know...crazy right? Yes, I juggled all of this until I was no longer able to hold it all together. The rent began piling up after losing my childcare and eventually one of my jobs. Oh! did I mention I also worked two jobs? My security job was perfect for me and the crazy schedule as security is needed 24hours a day. Although I was good at multitasking I ended up losing my health, my home and my patience. I lived in a shelter with my 5 children for a year. Eventually I saved enough money to move out and to start my life over again. Through many nights of tear drenched writing, heart ache and pain from a 5yr marriage that ended in divorce and needing to work on my parenting skills I was just a hot mess. One thing is for certain...I never l lost my faith. It took me ten years to get my Degree but I did it. My family had to get therapy and prayer for traumatizing events but God kept his arms around us. Eventually I managed to get my life back on track and remarried.   Through the power of PRAYERS and keeping my faith in my heavenly Father he began to unveil my purpose. I had to go through homelessness so that I could tell someone else they can make it through. A snap shot of my story is written in my book, an Amazon Best Seller in 3 categories, The Audacity to Rise. I had begun to write my story and consulted with friends to get help on self publishing my book. I was led to Author

Latoya Boyd who is a great publicist who taught me about branding, social media, the importance content creation and visibility. She also taught me that my story would help others across the globe and that it will assist me in building my platform to become a speaker. She then introduced me to Tamika Ink who worked very closely with me to design my cover, back and interior. Please understand that I fought with my emotions as I wrote my story. Fear of being judged almost stopped me from publishing my first book. I had so many reasons to give up. Many people told me that I would not amount to anything but God was with me.

I have had my business for three and a half years now. In the first two years I only had a handful of clients each year. Then in 2017 I had a major hit to my finances and was laid off from my employer. I was devastated. However, I knew that I could not just sit there in my feeling and mourn the loss of a job. There were too many people in my family depending on me so I had to do something I was scared to do. My business was not generating enough income for me to sustain my family and I needed help. So I reached out to a Business Coach I had been admiring for a couple of years. It was the Women on the Rise Coach Marsha Guerrier.

It was difficult to let someone coach me at first because I had been burned by another person who was supposed to be my coach. I knew that I would not grow personally or professionally if I did not let go of the past. So I did through prayer and was guided to have a consultation with Marsha. I felt as if we were connected instantly. She worked with the budget I had, assessed me, and my business. Needless to say my business began to grow under her guidance and her coaching. Coaching is such an important part of growing in your career and business, I just can't stress it enough that you can't do it all alone. Since being coached I have had my website revamped to reflect my personality and business. In addition, I now have attractive brand colors, a Facebook group for Beyond A J.O.B. and a decent following whereas I did not have any of these things before. During my sessions I was able to gain phenomenal clarity in my business goals, developed packages for my clients to purchase, gain increased visibility and expand my services. I had no idea how safe I was playing until Marsha showed me a realistic plan that I could implement in real time and build upon for my next level in business. As result of going through coaching I have attained higher tier clients that have come back for repeated services. I increased revenue by 25% and have landed two small contracts worth thousands of dollars. In addition I have landed a new opportunity for employment and received a 12% raise in salary.

Years ago I made a promise to God and my family that once I was out of homelessness I would give back and help others in need. In November of 2017 Beyond A J.O.B. Inc partnered with the Davidson Community Center and gave 200 personal care packages to homeless women and female veterans. This story was featured on Bronx Net News Television. Shortly afterward in December of 2017 a building caught fire in the Bronx displacing about 22 families. I Donated coats and personal care packages to those families and was mentioned on major media markets in New York on channels 1, 2 and 4. I will continue to give as long as I have breath in my body. I did not want myself and my children to depend on the government to support us. Although most times I could not visually see my way out of the dark times in my life I had faith. Faith that with Prayer, Planning and Massive Action I would rise above my circumstances.

## *Who Are You Really?*

Many times we think that when looking for employment we have to match ourselves to the position. In a sense this is only part true. If you know exactly who you are and what you bring to the table then the matching part is easy. However, what if you do not match anything you apply for? What if you just hate the job you have always worked for half of your life? What if your past position was phased out to a lovely computerized system?

These are things many people think or worry about when it comes to their careers. So how can you overcome these feelings? First let's start off with a few questions:

1.  What types of positions have you held in the past?

2.  If you have never worked, have you volunteered your services in the community you where you live?

3.  What type of places did were you most comfortable working or volunteering in? ex. Retail or office

4.  What did you like about the job or position most?

5.  What didn't you like about the job?

6. What task would you do all day or for free because you love it so much?

7. Name about 5 things that you are skilled at doing.

8. What are the top three that people say that you are skilled at?

9. Has anyone ever paid you or offered to compensate you to perform a task for them outside of your job?

10. What are the types of jobs, positions or task that you absolutely hate? List as many as you like here.

## *Self-Assessment*

You are a whole person that is made up of several parts. There is no way to effectively choose a job that is right for you if you are only looking at what is being offered instead of who you are. Knowing who you really are and what is important to you is vital to the longevity and success of your career. Let's take a look at some of the main parts to focus on.

1. Skills: Name at least 5 skills you have and 5 skills you don't have but need or would like to learn.

a. _____

b. _____

c. _____

d. _____

2. People: Name 3 personality types you would love to work with, then next to it name 3 personality types you would stay away from. Make sure you write the reasons so you understand why you would want to work with the personality type or why you would not want to work with the type.

Love personality

a. _____

b. _____

c. _____

Non-Loveable personality

a. _____

b. _____

c. _____

d. _____

3.Purpose: What are the 5 areas that make you come alive, excited and motivate you?

a. _____

b. _____

c. _____

d. _____

e. _____

4. Now name the 5 areas that drain you, demotivate or turn you off.

a. _____

b. _____

c. _____

d. _____

5. Workplace: Name 5 places that have your dream jobs, describe what they look like, what culture would they have? Are they modern, family oriented, casual, etc.

a. _____

b. _____

c. _____

d. _____

e. _____

6. Knowledge: Write down the type of skills you have, used or demonstrated that opened up new career opportunities for you. At least 5.

a. _____

b. _____

c. _____

d. _____

e. _____

7. Salary: How much do you need to earn in order to sustain your quality of life? To keep your bills paid, save money and go out on occasion? What is your bottom line?

a. _____

b. _____

c. _____

8. Location: Where are you willing to work? Are you willing to relocate? Would you work a night, overnight or telecommute? Are you willing to work in an office setting, retail, factory or restaurant?

a. _____

b. _____

c. _____

d. _____

e. _____

Now when your diamond is complete you will then have a snap shot of all the qualities you are looking for in your next employment or opportunity. If you happen to find all the quality from your diamond exercise that you love then that is your dream job! At the very least you will want to have an opportunity that gives you most of what you are looking for to be fulfilled in your career. If you choose the later and it has only one or two things you enjoy chances are you will be running out of there to happy hour several times a week. Friday will seem so far away from Monday and heaven help you if you are on for the weekends.

# *Skills to Transfer*

What are transferrable skills? Transferrable skills are the skills that that you can apply to another task, position or opportunity. Take note of the skills that you have so that you talk about it in an interview:

1. Interpersonal Skills- This is basically how you interact and communicate with others.
2. Problem Solving Skills- Ability to identify a problem and solve the problem.
3. Leadership Skills- The ability to manage task, people or leading a project.
4. Technical Skills- Ability to work with machinery, computer programs or specific tools.
5. Flexibility Skills- Ability to adjust to various situations and environments.

# *Importance of Clarity*

Clarity is important in order to make change in your business, personal or career. Confidence says you know EXACTLY what you want in your life and career. When you have clarity you stand a higher chance to obtain the career you've always wanted. When you don't have clarity, experience that uneasy feeling of being lost.

A lack of clarity affects the people you meet, especially people in your network trying to help you find opportunities. If you don't know what you want, how can they refer you or help you with opportunities?

If you're a job seeker, what kind of job are you looking for? Why do you want that type of job? How do you see yourself in a few years working there? Do you see yourself happy and fulfilled?

Or if you're a professional, why do you want a career change? What do you want in your next job that your last one didn't offer? Is taking this change really what you want? If you had to think twice about your answer to those questions, you need to build up your clarity.

When you're out networking and doing interviews you must own who you are and what you want. Clarity is the foundation of a strong personal image and making a significant positive change in your career.

Here are the top four benefits having clarity:
1. You gain **more confidence.**
2. You become **more courageous**.
3. You become **more compelling at communicating.**
4. You gain a **concrete roadmap and plan.**

# *About Shaquan Hoke*

Shaquan Hoke, Founder and CEO of Beyond A J.O.B. Inc. - Career and Job Readiness Services, is an author, inspirational speaker, and training facilitator with over ten years of Professional Business Experience, Recruitment, Development, Sales and Job Readiness. Her company provides assistance in attaining the tools needed to gain employment or to map out a professional career, personal and business leadership coaching, inspirational speaking and leadership training to organizations across the world. Shaquan's focus is on the quality of service provided, not the quantity of clients served. She views her clients as dynamic and diverse individuals who have ever-changing life-demands and evolving goals. No matter what your aspirations may be, Shaquan believes you can address your personal goals with a customized plan tailored for your success.

Shaquan has completed her first solo book, "Beyond A Job: Seven Steps to Create & Move Into Your Vision"; which details her transition to true freedom through the application of Prayer. Shaquan is a co-author in her second book titled, "Through The Valley". She also has a Planner for Job and Opportunity Seekers who want to stat organized. Books are found on Amazon and www.beyondajob.net. Shaquan walks in her divine purpose daily as a servant and leader to empower others to become the best person that they can be and ultimately fulfill their divine destiny in life.

Let's Get Social! Connect with Bestselling Author Shaquan Hoke online at:
Visit website or email beyondajobnyc@gmail.com
Instagram - @ShaquanHoke www.instagram.com/shaquanhoke/
Twitter - @AuthorShaquanH www.twitter.com/AuthorShaquanH
Facebook - www.facebook.com/authorShaquanHoke/

# RISE SIMPLIFIED BUSINESS PLAN
## EXERCISE 2

## PRODUCT - SERVICE

Please describe:

1. What products/services do you offer now, how it differs from the past and what you will offer going forward?

2. What needs or problems your product/service addresses for the marketplace and how?

3. The features and benefits (customer viewpoint) of your product/ service.

4. How your product/service is different from others on the market

# Chapter 3

Natasha Nurse

*What Entrepreneurship Means to Me*

If I had to pick one word to represent entrepreneurship, the word I would choose would be tenacity. Every day I wake up knowing it is a blessing that I never take for granted. How does entrepreneurship make me feel? Hungry. I am eager to work, learn, and evolve as a woman, a wife, and entrepreneur. Essentially, entrepreneurship makes up a big part of my inner fire that drives me to go after my dreams. Growing up, I always wanted to do a lot. There was never a day in my life where I said I wanted to do one thing. Things never changed as I grew up. There is so much I want to do and see in this world and I am hungry to make strides as a woman, as a Jamaican-American, and as a business person. Who doesn't feel this way?

## *What Do I Do?*

Entering the world of entrepreneurship meant that I needed to be doing something that I loved and truly moved me. For me, there is nothing more compelling than the empowerment of young girls and women. I wanted to design my business around projects and ventures that helped women and young girls become better content creators, presenters, public speakers, event organizers and anything else they desire. As a coach, I am a cheerleader and a drill sergeant for my clients who need a push to be more organized, determined, and resourceful to transform their personal and professional lives. My consultation services are used specifically on projects and ventures that resonate with what is important to me and the female community. Whether I am working on social media needs, event production, or content creation these services are surrounded around the idea of promoting the idea that women are completely capable of doing what we want in this world. Who runs the world?

# *Early Life*

I can only smile when I think back on what led me to creating my coaching and consulting company Dressing Room 8. Growing up in the concrete jungle of Manhattan, I was the girl who spent most of my time by myself. I was always reading a book, writing a poem, or indulging my passion for television programs and film. I didn't begin to build a supportive group of friends until much later in life. School was something that I learned to master early on. I remember studying at 2 AM when I was in second grade. Yes, I was that girl. I was the one who always made sure my teachers knew my name and why I was excited to be in their class. I was also the one who asked for extra credit assignments and extra summer reading. This behavior served me well. In high school, I maintained a 4.0 for 4 years and graduated with the third highest grade point average.

When I headed off to Pennsylvania State University, I was so confident that I was going to continue my stellar academic record. Sadly, that was not the case at all. In my first semester, I received my first C and I was floored. How could this have happened to me? Grades like that were given to other people, not me. Honestly, this obstacle was one of the greatest things to happen to me (in addition to meeting my Husband at school). This shock forced me to think about my future in a whole new way. I was majoring in Animal Science and it was re-emphasized to me from my classmates, professors, and school administrators just how difficult it is to become a veterinarian. Since I was little, I was obsessed with animals. I always loved spending time with them, but did I really want to be a vet that treated them? No, not really. When I became very honest with myself, I realized that I could be passionate about animals and continue to be an animal activist without having to become a veterinarian. This was the first pivot in my life. It was a moment in my life where I gave myself permission to change my career trajectory on my terms irrespective of what others thought or said. So, I began to sign up for business and legal courses for the rest of my time at Pennsylvania State University. Guess what happened next? I loved the new coursework. It sparked a yearning inside to consider the opportunity to become a lawyer. Why? As a lawyer, I knew that I could practice law and enjoy this new path for myself. Or, I could use my law degree in a non-traditional career and still benefit from the training and knowledge I learned in law school. Turns out, I was very right. Despite all the discouragement about going to law school, I was proudly admitted to New York Law School in 2008, just in time for the financial crisis in the US. This wasn't ideal timing to begin law school or rack up large law school debt, but I made the most of it. I graduated in 2011, successfully passed the New York State Bar Exam, and went on a twisty career path as a non-traditional attorney. In a legal educational sales role, it became apparent to me that I needed to figure what was next for my career. I needed to take control and become very clear and mindful about my career. This is how Dressing Room 8 was born. The road was not direct, but I wouldn't take back any part of it. This journey led me to living a life that makes me smile with joy and gratefulness each day.

## *Life Balance*

Most people in my life always ask me, how do I manage everything in my life? My typical response is: *People make time for what they want to make time for.* My business isn't something I need to do, but it is something that I deeply love. It is the highlight of the beginning, middle, and end of the day. Creating content that inspires or motivates a woman to take a singing lesson, write a book, launch an online course, or start a live-stream on Facebook, gives me life. The best way to achieve harmony (not balance) in your life comes down to this checklist that I live by:

1. Set the intention of the day with your needs
2. Think about 3 things you are grateful for every day
3. Write or type your daily checklist you want to accomplish for the day
4. Celebrate every victory you have (no matter how small or how large)
5. Read at least 15 minutes every day (the more you read, the more you evolve)
6. Discuss your journey with those who want the best for you
7. Cut out the negative and complaining people in your network immediately
8. Decide what living your best life means and be determined to live the way you want

## *Secrets of Success*

It is up to you to decide what it takes to be successful. I have defined success with these key principals:

1. Living with clarity, confidence and purpose
2. Learning something new and meeting someone new every day
3. Never giving up on being happy
4. Living on your own terms not the opinions or needs of others
5. Encouraging the world to be a better place for all of us
6. Accepting that failure doesn't exist
7. Embracing who you are and being authentic to who you are
8. Controlling the words you think and speak – words always matter!

## *What Makes Me Successful*

To live my best life and feel successful, I must pay attention to the Holy Trinity of Life:

1. Mind – Focusing on books, podcasts, articles and networking events that help me evolve as a better person, wife, woman, activist and business person.
2. Body – My health has been more important than ever before. Recently being diagnosed with Hypothyroidism has forced me to prioritize what I put in my body and how often I move my body every day.
3. Soul – Growing up in a Christian culture, showed me that spiritual enhancement and growth helps me feel more grounded and centered in my life. Enjoying the ministry of spiritual leaders like Joyce Meyer and Steven Furtick really goes a long way for feeling empowered and supported in my daily life.

## *Goal Setting*

The journey of entrepreneurship is such a surprising path that so many people can't seem to get enough of. Usually, the business you envision in the beginning ends up being different than the business you end up with months or years later. For me, I focused Dressing Room 8 on consultation services, but when I added coaching services in 2016, my goals shifted to that side of the business. Additionally, starting the WokeNFree podcast with my husband and hosting Our Voices on 90.3 WHPC helped spark my passion for pursing more media related activities. Being a part of more podcasts, radio programming, and television programs is the bigger focus for me right now. Being a public media person helps me to spread my message and platform in a whole new way.

## *Resources*

I was taught at a young age that people should embrace education and knowledge. I truly believe no one lives their life thinking that they knew too much or learned too much. Who would really say this? I enjoy waking up each morning seeking out knowledge to feed my mind, body, or soul. Do you know what I love to do? Share knowledge and resources that have made a tremendous difference in my life.

Here are resources that have transformed my life:

**Books**

- **The Secret by Rhonda Byrne** – This book will teach you the mindset techniques needed to accomplish every dream or ambition you have.
- **The Universe has Your Back by Gabrielle Bernstein** – Did you know that you are supported by the universe? How different would your life look if you knew this to be true? Read this book to transform your outlook on your life.
- **Who Moved My Cheese? by Spencer Johnson, M.D.** – People truly struggle with loss and transitions in their life. Why? They have not read this book, or they do not put the book principles into practice.
- **Create or Hate by Dan Norris** – Are you on this earth to create or to hate? Read this book and you will see what thoughts and actions are needed to be a creator or hater.
- **Show Your Work by Austin Kleon** – If you are an artist or creating content that the world needs to see, then what are you doing to make sure it is seen? This book helps you see how you are completely in control of this reality.
- **Year of Yes: How to Dance It Out, Stand In the Sun, and Be Your Own Person by Shonda Rhimes** – Are you saying yes to the universe? If not, what would your life look like if you spent a year saying yes? This book shares the journey of Shonda Rhimes' year of yes.
- **You Are a Badass: How to Stop Doubting Your Greatness and Start Living an Awesome Life by Jen Sincero** – Doubting

yourself is a complete waste of time. Don't believe me? Read the book.

**Podcasts** – There are so many podcasts that you can enjoy but here are three that you will adore!

- **WokeNFree** – If you haven't listened to this podcast, you will love it. I am not saying this because of all the blood, sweat and tears that go into making it. But, listening to my husband and I as we tackle on relationships, technology, marriage, ghosts, politics, aliens, music, culture, and everything in between will literally make you smile and laugh each episode. Do you see why you need to join the WokeNFree Nation?
- **Entrepreneurs on Fire** – I will sum up this podcast in one word: Dope.
- **The GaryVee Audio Experience** – The name of this podcast is very well suited. Everything Gary Vaynerchuk offers is an experience we can all benefit from.

**Influencers & Thought Leaders** – Here are some people that truly inspire me to be the best version of myself! I would also say, I am inspired by people who are determined to live their best life. People who authentically go after their dreams and encourage others to do the same truly motivate me. If you don't know any of these people, use Google and learn about the positive changes they are putting out into the world.

- Michael Eric Dyson
- Dr. Cornel West
- Gary Vaynerchuk
- Steven Furtick
- Joyce Meyer
- Michelle & Barack Obama
- Rhonda Byrne

- Cory Booker
- Issa Rae
- Shonda Rhimes
- Gabrielle Bernstein
- Tony Robbins
- Zig Ziglar
- Oprah Winfrey
- Barbara Corcoran
- Amandla Stenberg
- Cynthia Nixon
- Dan Norris
- Maddy Jones
- Marcia McNair
- Kahlil Nurse
- Marsha Guerrier (the reason you are reading this book!)
- Featured Women of the Sistas On Fire IRL Series
- Long Island Girl Talk Participants

## *Last Minute Thoughts*

Thank you for reading my story and picking up this book. By doing so I know that you are ready for transformation and innovation in your life. If you want to be an entrepreneur, go out into the world and figure out what that means for you. If you want to change your career, be bold and daring enough to explore new opportunities and meet new people so you can make that career change. If you want to travel, don't say you can't while secretly hoping to do so. Buy the ticket and see the wonders the world has to offer. The point is to do what you want and live your best life. Don't be the person who stands in your own way of the blessings coming your way.

No matter what you decide to do in life, don't forget the following 8 rules:

1. Life is too short not to live your best life each day
2. Surround yourself with people that make you better not worse
3. Maya Angelou taught us that when people show who they are, we should believe them – stop questioning what is right in front of you
4. Learn something new and meet someone new every day – This is my life motto and it has made my life more exciting and interesting in ways I could never have imagined
5. Always be kind to yourself – there is only one version of yourself in this world
6. Open your mind to what the universe has in store for you
7. You are more capable than you think you are
8. Find a reason to smile and embrace joy as much as possible

Enjoy the checklist of success I have provided below and feel free to contact me on www.dressingroom8.com or Natasha@dressingroom8.com. I look forward to hearing from you soon!

# Dressing Room 8

## DAILY EMPOWERMENT CHECKLIST

- ✓ Smile at yourself in the mirror

- ✓ Find something that you're grateful for (small or big)

- ✓ Notice negative people or events around you, and walk away

- ✓ Close your eyes and think of a time you were happiest or most excited

- ✓ Make sure your posture is straight

- ✓ Think of someone who cares for you and send them a text or email

- ✓ Remind yourself that there is always someone in the world who wishes they had your problems

### Facts to Remember

- ✓ Your life reflects what you think in your mind

- ✓ Your words have power in your life

- ✓ Say yes to yourself and to the universe

# About Natasha Nurse

Natasha started Dressing Room 8 to provide a web-based resource where women can gain personal and professional empowerment through her fashion and lifestyle focused blog, which also includes consultation and coaching services. Dressing Room 8 helps women learn how to think with clarity, dress with confidence, and live with purpose.

Not one to stay idle, Natasha loves to keep a full calendar. Aside from running Dressing Room 8, Natasha is an Adjunct Professor at Nassau Community College where she teaches Introduction to Women's Studies. She is the Lifestyle Editor for Plus Model Magazine. She is also the Program Coordinator for Long Island Girl Talk, a Long Island non-profit organization that teaches teenage girls how to produce, direct and star in their own television show about girl issues in their communities. Recently, she partnered with her husband to create the new podcast WokeNFree, while becoming the host of Our Voices on 90.3 WHPC around the same time. She is also the Press Director for Sistas On Fire, a newsical where the personal becomes the political, when four passionately-opinionated African American women speak their minds on the aftermath of Hurricane Katrina, Black Lives Matter, missing women and girls, racial stratification on Long Island, sexual exploitation, black-on-black crime, and male/female relationships. These topics are addressed in a soul-stirring mix of song, dance, spoken word poetry, and prose. Lastly, she is the proud creator and host of the online Sistas On Fire IRL series.

Follow Natasha on Facebook, Instagram, Twitter, Pinterest, YouTube, and Google Plus.

# RISE SIMPLIFIED BUSINESS PLAN
## EXERCISE 3
## MARKET & INDUSTRY – TARGET MARKET

Please describe:

1. The size of your industry and market by both revenue and number of firms

2. The characteristics of this industry and market, such as growth trends, units sold and employment

3. The industry, product/service, years in business, revenue, employee size, public/private status of the general market and of the specific group(s) you are targeting -- Identify the top two or three segments of the market you intend to focus on in the immediate future. (A well-defined target market that you can effectively serve is more appealing than a huge less well-defined target market.)

4. Where your customers are located – global, U.S., other country, state, metro area

# Chapter 4

Nina Monique Spain

The Corporate Rebel

Being an entrepreneur makes me feel empowered because I'm in charge of myself and business. After having to report to other people for so long I now feel independent and that sense of independence pushes me to go even further. I also love being an entrepreneur because it allows me to take risk and step outside of my comfort zone which I love because I don't like following the norm or rules, I like to be and enjoy being rebellious and following my own path. I'm confined to Corporate America for 10 hours or more during the week so the moment I can be free and be myself I take advantage of it which is how my first business Nina Monique Voluptuous Boutique came about. I realized that there is way more to life than sitting at an office desk being used to build and maintain someone else's business. So once those feelings began to surface I decided it was time to take action and apply what I learned from my corporate job and redirect my focus into becoming an entrepreneur.

## *Day One*

One day I was watching VH1's Single Ladies and the idea about starting my own clothing line popped up in my head. I wanted to be like the character Valerie Stokes played by Stacey Dash. What intrigued me about Valerie's character is that she was a designer, a store owner and an entrepreneur with her owned shop in Atlanta, Ga. Her shop was a clothing store for women and it was also a place for women to hang out with their girlfriends and I absolutely loved the idea of having a place where women can go try on clothes, shop, have garments designed just for their body type, mingle and feel safe and comfortable. During the time I watched the show I was also annoyed with the lack of style for plus size clothing so one day after work I went to pick up some sketch books along with coloring pencils from Toys R Us and then made a to trip to some fabric stores to pick up a few fabric swatches. Once I got home I started sketching, I came up with ideas for different styles of clothing and after accumulating about 6 books filled with ideas for garments I said okay God what's next? Next thing you know I'm meeting people at work who have their own businesses in different industries telling me about their journey of entrepreneurship and advising me to sit down with an attorney to get my business incorporated, so that's just what I did. I also met a designer through a co-worker by the name of Tiffany who is from Harlem. She helped me develop different looks for my first product line. I'm grateful for Tiffany because there were a lot of things I really didn't know about fashion until she showed me, I greatly appreciate her time and dedication to helping me get the initial designs, garments and the brand together.

## *Research*

I started doing research to find an attorney in NYC and after about a month or so I finally found one in lower Manhattan on Wall Street in New York City. After a few meetings with the attorney we started discussing how I wanted my business to be formed, normally attorneys charge a consultation fee but the attorney I worked with charged me very little or nothing at all because she liked my professionalism, my drive and the fact that I knew a great deal about the different ways I can form my business from being a Compliance Officer. My experience in banking my background as a Compliance Officer served its purpose. But for those who may not have a Compliance background I would advise you do a lot of research about the different ways to form a business and the documents that are required. There's a lot to learn about the language that goes into an LLC agreement or Operating Agreement especially when it comes to ownership structure, shares, capital contribution, voting rights, dissolving a business and more depending on what type of business you may have and how many people are part of that business. The internet is a good place to find information, websites like Legal Zoom is one place or just Google

Limited Liability Company, Partnership, Sole Proprietorship, and Corporation, etc. but I also advise that once you do your research you should sit down face to face with an attorney if possible because in my opinion sitting down face to face is just better and it allows you to develop a better business relationship. I would also advise you to come with questions because when it comes to the part about taxes it can be very confusing. You may have to meet a few times a week, I had to see my attorney at least 3 or 4 times a week because I would only get about an hour or an hour and a half with him due to my work schedule and sometimes it would be after 6:30pm so everything pretty much took time. Not to mention I had to work around my paycheck because those documents can be costly even on Legal Zoom once again depending on what type of business you're forming.

After working with my attorney for quite some time Nina Monique Voluptuous Boutique was born on October 29, 2012 as I like to say, and with this business it was all about Nina Monique Spain, something that I loved and it was completely different from my corporate 9 to 5 so I was pleased. I was able to sketch, design, be creative and pick out prints, materials, have different styles of clothing including sexier fashions for the plus size women, as well as career and casual pieces. I use to get so mad and ask why did I get into banking and now I see why. My career gave me the foundation to understand the back-end of running a business. Once I received my corporate book (you get this after forming your company) from my attorney that included the LLC Agreement she and I drafted Articles of Incorporation, and other documents I signed as sole owner and CEO. The strongest most delightful feeling came over me because just that process alone was a lot of work and I made it. It was a huge investment, and it took up most of my time but no regrets because that was only the beginning. This moment provided so many other wonderful opportunities afterwards.

# *Find a Mentor*

Although I was super excited about forming the company this really wasn't my first time experiencing this feeling because when I was growing up my grandmother introduced me to entrepreneurship at the age of six and I shadowed her up until the age of seventeen when she sold her business. Even though my name wasn't on any of the documents of ownership for her night club she made sure I knew I was her little business partner by including me in most of her journey in maintaining and running her business. My grandmother wanted me to have a fun childhood but she also wanted me to learn about entrepreneurship. Even though she knew I wouldn't understand most it because of my age but she knew one day I would possibly use the skills she taught me.

My grandmother included me in just about the entire process of her business. She had me tagging along from the beginning, starting with me going with her to meetings to speak with the previous owner whom she was purchasing the club from and going to meet with her attorney's to discuss leasing and various contracts. I literally had no idea what my grandmother and her attorney were talking about because I was too young but I remember her saying to me "Nina, always read your contracts thoroughly. What you don't understand ask questions and if you still don't understand the answer, don't sign anything until you do". I also went with her to the municipal building in downtown Paterson to pick up her liquor license, she took me to the bank with her to open up a business checking account, and when she finally opened up Wayside Palace it was the best feeling ever. She took me out to get seafood to celebrate and I remember the smile on her face and how she hugged, squeezed and kissed me while saying "We did it poops".

Every Saturday morning my mother and grandmother would get up to go clean up her night club and of course I had to go because there was no one around to babysit me. While we were there, I would assist my grandmother with keeping her books up-to-date for the accountant; she showed me how to count money from the register, check inventory etc... I didn't get paid for it but I learned a lot and didn't realize it until I got older when it was time for me to sit down in front of an attorney to form my business Nina Monique Voluptuous Boutique. I wanted to be just like my grandmother when I grew up a strong, independent, classy and a well respected business owner who everyone ran to for personal and business advice. I can say some of that came true for me. My grandmother laid out the blueprint and exposed me to the good, bad and hard side of being an entrepreneur. Every day I wish she could see the impressions she left behind but I will keep her legacy alive by doing what she did and that's teaching my kids about entrepreneurship when I decide to have them.

Entrepreneurship has its down side as well which I have also experienced but for the most part I understand it's a part of my journey. I'm still loving every minute of it because with every low comes a high. I can recall at one point I wanted to walk away from my clothing line because it was just too costly and was becoming unbearable to manage because I was investing so much of my money into my business and not seeing anything come back. My bank account was drying out and I personally was becoming mentally drained because everything was so expensive, especially to have pieces of clothing made including samples, getting a website, maintaining my mailbox, doing small photo shoots etc... all while still paying my personal bills, paying for my commute to get to work every day in NYC, and maintaining a roof over my head. Honestly, I just wanted to drop Nina Monique Voluptuous Boutique and just when I was about to give up on my business I received an opportunity to appear on an internet radio show called "Thick World Radio" to talk about my clothing line and from there things began to shift.

# *Lessons Learned*

When thoughts of wanting to give up arrive it is important to think about how far you have come and what you have accomplished. For me personally, I instantly reflect back to my grandmother and how I watched her fight through the challenges and obstacles she endured while trying to run a successful business. What I learned from her is to never give up because you come too far, invested too much time and more than likely a whole lot of money into your business to turn around and say I'm not doing this anymore because of difficult moments or challenging experiences. Instead of looking at how difficult that moment may be, look at what you have already accomplished and understand you're learning a lesson from this experience and use that as motivation to keep pushing forward. It's important that you remind yourself of why you decided to become an entrepreneur in the first place and block out everything else. Having that mindset keeps me feeling empowered because from it I embark on new milestones which continue to give me the fuel I need to thrive, remain ambitious and happy about being an entrepreneur. If I would've given up there's no way I would've met another very good friend of mine name Katia Page who has her own non-profit organization called The Lipedema Queen. org. Through her I met the host of "Thick of World Radio" Mr. Shawn M while attending her Curves Meets Confidence event and through Shawn I met the owner of In The Mixx Radio who goes by the name Cruize.

After appearing on "Thick World Radio" I was able to revisit my first love which is Media/Journalism, I really enjoyed making the appearance on "Thick World Radio" and so did the host because afterwards I was asked if I would be interested in joining the show as a co-host. I thought about it for a couple of days and made the decision to accept the offer. I decided to put my clothing line on hold to explore this opportunity because it was a break from the stress and a chance to allow everyone to find out who was Nina Monique. After I became a co-host of this radio show I felt the topics really were not for me so from there I made the choice to start my own internet radio show called The Nina Monique Show on In The Mixx Radio.

I love being a radio personality because I always wanted to be a Journalist, I like to write and talk about current events. I attended school in NYC for Journalism but didn't finish because I wanted to make money to support myself, therefore, I left school to begin working. What I didn't mention before I started my clothing line I started a magazine called Urban Youth Magazine which was designed to provide a platform for kids in the inner city to address the challenges, obstacles, lifestyles and issues they face on a daily basis. I always felt the media provided one-sided stories to the world and I wanted to do something to give the urban community the opportunity to tell their side of the story. So far hosting my own radio show earned myself and the show some awards from organizations for being an entrepreneur and topics covered on The Nina Monique Show.

## *Passion into Purpose*

My passion is to help people, I love to hear people stories, journey, struggles and the ways they overcame their dark times. I always felt my purpose in life was to somehow create a platform for people to get their stories out to help others who may be experiencing similar issues and The Nina Monique Show is where I can do it as well as touch on other topics such as domestic violence, bullying, entrepreneurship, current events, fashion and etc. When I get in front of the microphone I'm so happy and in my zone because it's my own platform where I can be myself and speak freely about the things that are important to me and possibly for other people. During my child and adulthood I experienced many trials and tribulations like fending off bullies, struggling with self-esteem, fitting in Corporate America, and surviving an unhealthy relationship, among many other challenges.

Most of my experiences caused me to be a resilient, blunt, bold, and confident and a hardworking corporate rebel who refuses to put limits on my dreams. Through my show I want to assist individuals such women, men and young adults who may be going through challenging times and want to hear some inspiring stories from guest I have on my show who come from different backgrounds and may be able to shed some light on how to overcome obstacles that some of my listeners may be experiencing. I not only want to provide a platform to discuss topics but I also want to encourage others to realize that we control our individual lives and have a voice along with the knowledge to create the change we want to see. It's important to always know at all times that you deserve the best out of life and to never settle or give up on your dreams.

Currently, I'm in the process of forming my second business which is an entertainment company that will have my radio show as a subsidiary and possibly two other business ventures I'm looking into. Having a radio show fuels my brain to keep going because I know there are so many places it can take me, it's truly different than what I'm used to and that's what keep me excited about having my own show.

There's so much that goes into a having a successful show from promoting, to booking guest, getting sponsors, dealing with annoying Publicists who don't like to communicate changes with your guest, guest arriving on time or something as simple as coming up with topics and questions. At times your guest may cancel at the last minute so you have to be prepared to switch up your whole program and do an entire show on your own or pull in last minute guest. This has happened to me a few times and although I would be steaming mad I always had to remind myself people can see me because I stream live so I must remain professional at all times because I am the face of my brand Nina Monique Voluptuous Boutique and The Nina Monique Show. Even if you don't have a brand named after you personally you must always remember you are a brand and your first impression can be your very last. So how you handle challenging guest, clients etc... is a reflection of your business. Be cautious. I can tell you I walked away from business owners because of bad energy, how situations were handled, right down to the tone in emails and phone calls. Remember I'm a Compliance Officer so I pay attention to a lot of details and so should others.

## *Balance vs. Harmony*

Having a business can take away from you feeling balance and your personal life usually suffers. Honestly, I don't really have much of a personal life because every part of me is just about dedicated to commuting, my full-time job and The Nina Monique Show. When I do have some time to myself normally I just turn off my cell phone and unplug from the world, I light candles and meditate. It helps me find harmony and it's the greatest thing I can do for myself, because during the week my life is busy with really no time to unwind. I also try to pamper myself by getting manicures, pedicures, my hair done, a massage or something where I can relieve some tension and stress. Normally on Friday after work and/or Saturday's after my show I also like to go out to dinner with my mother to Friday's for a meal and drink then afterwards go get some ice cream and enjoy my life. I used to take for granted living in New Jersey because it was slower than New York but now being older and commuting to NYC everyday when my bus gets on the NJ side of the Lincoln Tunnel and when it reaches my stop I'm so excited.

Traveling to Los Angeles, California is something else I love to do and one day I plan on relocating there. The plane ride to California is so relaxing I just sit back, look out the window, sip some water and fall asleep, when I get on the plane it's like my body takes a deep breath then sighs and from there on everything I know is forgotten until it's time to come back home.

You should always make time for yourself because your sanity is very important, a business can be stressful and you owe it to yourself to step away and take a vacation for a few days. I know someone who has a business that is very active and although he can't really take a vacation like he would prefer he has someone come in that he trust to take over for a week at least so he can rest up, clear his mind and come back feeling refreshed. Breaks and time away is very important I mean after all, you work hard why not give yourself some time to play. What you do in your leisure time is your business but it is very important you give yourself time to rest. Take time to get rejuvenated so you can come back and see things with a fresh pair of eyes and possibly a clearer mind.

Something else that helps me calm down is keeping a journal, it helps keep me sane, as I mentioned Journalism is my first love so writing and expressing my feelings is therapeutic to me. I do a lot of venting in my journals and they contain some things I don't share with others because they're personal feelings not just about my business but my life in general. I have in my journal passages containing goals, poetry, personal or business issues, work and etc for me keeping a journal is a form of solitude and can at times help me find peace, resolutions and closure to some issues I maybe experiencing at the moment.

My circle of friends is very small because honestly I can barely keep up with myself so to have a huge circle of friends is not possible for me. I have about maybe five or six friends that I go out with or invite over my house for dinner who are all also entrepreneurs. We talk about what's going on with our business and try to be an ear to listen to each other and provide advice because we realize not everyone can relate to our experiences and struggles. One of my good friends Leslie Garcia is a Clinical Social Worker based in New York City who specializes in mental health and wellness for women entrepreneurs, she started her business Counseling Space to help women who are struggling behind the scenes with the mental challenges that are often associated with business ownership and professional leadership. Whenever I get stressed out she is normally the first person I communicate with because she is a professional and she truly finishes my sentences when I'm talking to her about the issues I may be facing with my business. I have 4 other friends that I vent to because I feel safe talking to them and to be truthfully honest you need that, you will need someone to talk to because being a business owner can become very overwhelming and there are people like my friend Leslie who specialize in working with entrepreneurs.

## *Set Goals to Keep Pushing*

One of my biggest goals was to have the freedom to express myself whether through clothing or writing but I never imagined it would be through radio. That honestly took me by surprise. I went from having a clothing line to being the host of my own show but my main goal still is to encourage, empower and inspire others as well as speak freely about issues that are dear to my heart. Another goal I have is generating multiple streams of revenue through my brand and currently I'm sketching some t-shirts along with other merchandise to have some sassy and bold statements written on them to start selling to the public. Eventually I would like to somehow step into TV and host my own talk show almost like the show The Real or possibly revisit having a magazine but more than likely it would be a digital publication because there are very few surviving paper magazines due to technology. I personally believe, in due time everything will fall in place and align itself, I'm putting in the work, learning lessons, meeting new people, receiving awards for The Nina Monique Show and I'm truly enjoying this journey. I can say a good amount of goals I've had I achieved and the biggest one I accomplished is having my own platform and being able to tell my story to empower, inspire and encourage others to never give up.

At times I'm amazed at what I have accomplished because I didn't finish college and I hear people say to others all the time if you don't obtain a college degree you won't get anywhere in life and truthfully that is something I just don't believe. I think a college degree is great to have but at the same time there are plenty of people who don't have a degree and are very successful. I personally feel everyone must find their path in life, my journey was long, having to go through banking and to be where I am now but I see how my journey plays a major part in me being a radio personality.

# *About Nina Monique Spain*

Prior to creating The Nina Monique Show, Nina Monique worked in Investment Banking for various well known top tier investment firms in NYC. However, after a while she felt unappreciated and realized its more to life than sitting at an office desk being used to build and maintain someone else's business. Once those feelings surfaced Nina decided to take what she learned and redirect her focus into becoming an entrepreneur.

Hailing from Paterson, NJ, Nina Monique is a relatable woman. During her child and adulthood she experienced many trials and tribulations like fending off bullies, struggling with self-esteem, fitting in Corporate America, and surviving an unhealthy relationship, among many other challenges. However she realizes most of these experiences caused her be a resilient, blunt, bold, confident and a hardworking corporate rebel who refuses to put limits on her dreams.

"Through The Nina Monique Show I not only want to provide a platform to discuss topics but I also want to encourage others to realize we control our individual lives and have voices along with the knowledge to create the change we want to see. It's important you always remain positive, humble and know at all times you deserve the best out of life. Never settle or give up on your dreams."

**Contact Nina:**

FB Page: The Nina Monique Show
Instagram: theninamoniqueshow
Youtube: The Nina Monique Show
https://www.ninamonique.com/home

# RISE SIMPLIFIED BUSINESS PLAN
## EXERCISE 4

## CAPITALIZATION – FINANCIALS

Please describe:

1. How much the founder(s) invested in the business and what it was used for (The more you've invested, the easier it is to attract financing.)

2. How much capital you need, what you plan to spend it on (expansion, risk cushion, covering seasonality/cycles)), specific uses, and how fast you will use it and where will you get it?

3. The "reasons behind the numbers" and how they were calculated (e.g., assume sell 1000 units first month at $5 each, with 4% projected increase each month, etc.)

4. How many units you need to sell at what price to cover your fixed and variable expenses (i.e., what is your break-even point?)

# Chapter 5

*Kia Daniels-Peck*

*Reflections*

# *Reflections*

My name is Kia Daniels-Peck, daughter of Scherry Smiley and John Lee Daniels. I grew up in a 2-family brownstone in Brooklyn, NY and the second eldest of 5 siblings (2 girls and 3 boys). Although I did not grow up with my Dad in the house, both parents held jobs and enjoyed a comfortable lifestyle. My family worked in prestigious industries like the military, U.S. Postal Service, real estate and banking.

Growing up in my house, we were taught very early on the importance of hard work and that money does not grow on trees. I was told that hard work and a good job with benefits is the key to freedom and independence. Even as teens, my sister and I were required to contribute $50 a month towards the phone bill, so at the age of 16 I found my first job through a High School co-op program that allowed me to meet my monthly obligation at home. While this hardly felt like freedom and independence, I knew there must be a lesson in here somewhere. And, while our parents taught us the importance of hard work and earning a living, no one taught me the most important key to achieving financial independence (i.e) saving and investing. And, boy would I learn this the hard way!

"GOD is fighting for YOU in ways you don't even know!"

**Self-Reflection:**
Can you think of your first experience with money and how you were taught about money?

_____

_____

_____

_____

Those early years of employment put me in the position to be hired as a full-time employee right out of High School. I will never forget my first boss, Ben Ozir, President and CEO of Stentor's/PSV. He was an older, well-dressed, Jewish man who hired me for my first job working in the repair department. Ben was a stern man that ran a tight nit business. After hiring me from the co-op program in H.S. they moved me into an Administrative position which allowed me to learn the business inside out: customer service, sales, meeting and greeting clients visiting the showroom. I loved the experience and I was open to learning all aspects of the business and he was willing to teach me. Over a relatively short period of time (one year to be exact), I worked my way up the ranks of becoming a manager with five men under my direct supervision. This was particularly challenging and rewarding for me because I was the youngest within the company and the only black female out of 25 employees.

It wasn't easy moving up the ranks, but with my effort and skills he noticed something different about me. However, as much as this prepared me to manage and supervise others, which was extremely challenging, it still didn't prepare me to control my finances. Even at this point I still did not have a checking-savings account until the day Ben took me out in the field with him to meet with a client. Afterwards, we stopped at Citibank off 57$^{th}$ Street and Park Avenue to deposit the company funds from the day before. He would always encourage me to save money. As we walked into the bank, he turned to me and asked: "Do you have an account and if so, how much are you saving and with which bank?" It was such an awkward moment I just stared into space trying to come up with an excuse, not knowing how to respond to such an easy question. I asked myself.... "Why, don't you have an account?" After dying of embarrassment, I shamefully admitted that I did not have one. Once I told him, to my surprise he said "ok, I will open one for you today while we are here." The fact that he took the time to educate, equip and empower me to do better with my money made me feel independent and powerful. As a final gesture to show how important saving and money management was to him, he deposited $100 into my account and instructed me to start saving $50-$100 each pay period. I know that you are probably thinking...she should have millions saved buy now. Well, sadly I did not follow Ben's golden rule. I was stubborn and just did not listen...ugh.... If I knew what I know now, I would be a millionaire. By the age of 18, I was making a decent salary, but as soon as I made a deposit, the money was being spent less than a day after. Unfortunately, the words of my old boss and that valuable lesson he tried to teach me was lost on a young person who wasn't ready to take control of her finances. Instead my finances took control of me.

*"Always help someone. You might be the only one that does!"*

**Self-Reflection:**

Do you remember the first time you opened a bank account? Who took you and how did you feel?

_____

_____

_____

_____

As the years flew by, I never manage to save. Now, here I was at the age of 20... and rapidly heading in the wrong direction. My spending habits grew out of control and soon I was introduced to credit cards. I didn't just have one card, no, no, no; I had cards for all the major stores- Macy's, Lord & Taylor, Bloomingdale's and Nordstrom. At the age of 20, now living with my grandmother in Harlem, with no real financial responsibilities I became careless with my spending. All cards were charged to the maximum and I was in debt approximately $10,000.00.

To make matters even worse, a friend asked if I would co-sign a loan, so he could buy a car. Foolishly, I agreed without the slightest understanding of the consequences and responsibilities that came with such a big commitment. One day I received a collect call from Jessup Correctional Institution. It was my so-called friend advising he had been arrested for trafficking drugs and that the car was being held in the pound. To make a long story short this individual got caught trafficking drugs from state-to-state in the vehicle without my knowledge. I was so scared, angry and embarrassed, I never told my parents. I had to take a bus to Maryland then have my brother drive to the facility to claim the vehicle from the pound. I was not prepared to deal with this at all. In the interim, I was not questioned by the police, thank GOD! Furthermore, I was not financially stable to take on a car note, so I negotiated with the bank in an effort to settle the case, however the bank wanted the car note paid in full and was not interested in my problems. This was not good. It affected my credit with the banks and my fico score. I was screwed and had no choice but to file bankruptcy. So, there I was, devastated and broke, standing before a Judge in downtown Brooklyn courts filing Chapter 7. But that wasn't even enough to make me stop spending. Things were going to get worse.

*"GOD will take you from the PIT to the PALACE."*

**Self-Reflection:**

Have you put yourself in a position where you allowed someone else to destroy your financial wealth?

_____

_____

_____

_____

# *New Beginnings*

After filing for bankruptcy, I was ready for a new beginning in my life and my finances. In 1988, I met my husband. He was such a breath of fresh air and it was high time I had a frank conversation with myself about who I am, where I have been and where I want to be in the future. I was able to honestly confront all my mistakes and ready to get my life back on track. Dwight helped me look for my own apartment and even helped furnish it. I have always earned a living, but I never saved and that is something I was committed to working on. I started small by limiting my traveling (which was a huge cost), eliminate all credit cards and pay for things with cash.

As my life was getting back on track, I decided to buy a Nissan Pathfinder. I was single with my own apartment and now I needed a vehicle to get around. The first couple of months were manageable, but once again my spending habits got out of control and I was missing monthly payments. After a year of being in possession of the car, I fell behind in my payments. One Saturday morning I woke up and my car was gone! Yup, it was repossessed! It sounds horrible to say. Ugh....word of advice.... pay now or you will pay double later. Let's just say I had to come up with the money to take it out of the storage as well as the back payments for the loan. Thankfully my husband, then boyfriend, was kind enough to help me out and rescue me from the situation. But was that enough for me to get my finances in order?

*"You can always take the easy way out and give up, but real strength comes when you decide to keep pushing forward no matter what the circumstances are."*

**Self-Reflection:**
Are you still living the fast life? What will it take to really change you?

_____

_____

_____

_____

## *The Breakthrough*

Financially I needed more but getting a second job was not an option. I just felt that wasn't the route for me as I was the Diva of Corporate America. I always had the mindset of an entrepreneur, I just wasn't sure what I would be doing. I worked my way up the ladder and became Executive Assistant to the Vice President & General Counsel of Brooks Brothers. I was the first African-American woman to work in the Executive Office. Things were great, but the income was not, I NEEDED MORE...

The financial crisis of 2007-2008, also known as the global financial crisis is considered by many economists to have been the worst financial crisis since the Great Depression of the 1930s. Times were hard for everyone. Numerous layoffs, foreclosures, deaths and so much more. I knew it was time for change. In 2009, after being introduced by a good friend I decided to join Primerica Financial Services, Inc. Once I learned I can generate income by transforming my life and the lives of others I was all in. I secured licenses to operate in New York, Maryland and Georgia. I was promoted several times and eventually became District Leader. I believed this venture could sustain me and I decided to do it full time. Of course my family was confused and my husband not happy. I left a steady income with benefits without consulting and discussing this life changing decision with my husband. Wrong move ladies.... trust me.

The first year went well. I was able to keep up with the bills and maintain my life. The thought of working from home seemed easy since I was calling my own shots, no early morning hustle on the MTA and nobody telling me what I could and could not do. I was a made BOSS, at least that's what I thought. My husband allowed me to work from home for 3 years (yes, I said allowed – it's not easy for your spouse to hold it ALL down after being put into a position he was not ready to handle, but he did it for me).

*"Be PREPARED for what you are PRAYING for!"*

**Self-Reflection:**

How has your actions with finances impacted those closest to you?

_____

_____

_____

_____

During those 3 years, the financial burden became a wedge in our marriage. Tension was high and once again I did not follow through with my responsibilities. I fell into a deep depression with my personal life which was compounded by my Primerica business. I was stuck – at least I thought I was. All I had to do was to refocus on my goals and work my business like a job, so it could pay me like it was a business. I got sick and tired of being sick and tired of allowing my income to dictate how I live, what I eat, even what I wear and places I visit.

I wanted FINANCIAL FREEDOM and I wanted it now. To accomplish this, I created a plan and I executed it. I opened up two mutual fund accounts and one 529 plan for my son. Within months

I paid off my debt and I became debt free and began saving $500 a month. Before I was making any real money, I made an investment in myself by showing up for training to learn as much about financial planning, connecting with mentors, which lead me to host weekly speaking engagements within Primerica and outside the company.

In 2015, I decided to swallow my pride and get back out in the working field. I immediately called my agency to alert them that I was back and ready to work. It wasn't easy, but I had to swallow my pride and make it do what it does! I knew getting back into the field would not jeopardize my position with Primerica. So, I did both. I worked full-time at a law firm and worked my business in the evening as well as weekends. It's not easy, but you do what you have to do when you have someone depending on your income. I am proud to say that I stuck with it and I am now a Regional Leader with Primerica working on becoming Regional Vice President.

Today, my professional career has allowed me to speak on various platforms such as churches, non-profit organizations, schools and numerous other organizations to educate, prepare and empowering others to make informed financial decisions. This is my passion today. There is a saying that I believe in; "Knowledge is Power", I know that if I hadn't experienced the grief, anger turmoil and shame that came from making poor financial decisions I do not believe I would be able to speak about this topic with passion and genuine concern to help others avoid financial pitfalls and lead a debt free life filled with happiness.

*"If there is anything in your life that is not the way you want it to be, you and only you are responsible for changing it. You must believe that it is up to you to create solutions to the challenges of life. Whether they are big or small, you're still responsible. Each time you give an excuse, you diminish your respect, your credibility, and your integrity. Each time you make an excuse, you reinforce your propensity to make even more excuses in the future, and excuse making becomes a habit.*
*~Tommy Newberry*

# *About Kia Daniels-Peck*

Kia Daniels-Peck was born in Brooklyn, NY; from a very young age she knew she wanted to be an Entrepreneur to help her community. During her career, she worked in the legal industry as an Executive Administrative Assistant for over 15 years with several top prestige law firms.

Kia legal experience was focused on litigation, corporate and governance matters including mergers and acquisitions, securities law issues and debt and equity financings. She assisted the Co-Chairman with clients ranging from small, closely-held family businesses to large entities and across a broad spectrum of businesses including magazine publishers, direct marketing companies, investment companies, restaurant and food service businesses, electronic distributors and manufacturing and service companies.

In 2008, she decided to transition into Finance. That is when she joined Primerica Financial Services, Inc. (www.primerica.com). Since she has joined the company Mrs. Peck has vigorously worked up the ranks to Regional Leader with the goal of becoming Regional Vice President. A particular focus of Mrs. Peck practice has been counseling and educating middle class families on all aspects of finance. Mrs. Peck has extensive experience addressing financial issues relating to the lifestyle of her clients.

In addition, as a consultant to many high net worth individuals she provides in-house consultation involving debt solutions, auto/home/life insurance, identity theft, legal protection (including Wills), long term care, investments and so much more. In 2016, Mrs. Peck took on another adventurous role at T&M Protection Services with the Investigations Unit (www.tmprotection.com). In the interim, she assists the Senior Vice President with various investigations as well as travel state-to-state to oversee audit procedures within numerous organizations.

Mrs. Peck is licensed with the Department of Insurance and a Member of the National Insurance Producer Registry (NIPR); Licensed States: NYC, MD and Georgia Affiliations & Organizations: Better Business Bureau, A.M. Best, American Council of Life Insurers and The Financial Industry Regulatory Authority.

# RISE SIMPLIFIED BUSINESS PLAN
## EXERCISE 5

## MARKETING & SALES

Please describe:

1. How you will communicate to your target market(s) about your product/service

2. The steps necessary to reach prospects and convert them to customers

3. The specific marketing mediums you will use to reach your customer (radio, TV, cable, newspaper, magazine, billboard/outdoor, Internet, e-mail, word of mouth, affiliates, partnerships, association involvement, packaging, brand name, reputation, etc.), along with how often each will be used and what it will cost (i.e., when, where, why, and how will you reach your target customer at what costs)

4. Why you chose these marketing avenues over others

# Chapter 6

*Terryl Ebony*

*Producing The Results I Want*

On Veterans Day of 1994, I gave birth to my "Why". HE wasn't planned, but I knew I needed to develop a plan if I was going to make it. I refused to succumb to being labeled and categorized as another sorry story statistic. My son became the primary reason for everything that happened in my life ever since. I had to raise Devon as a single mother. Although I had support, there were many things I had to do and figure out on my own. I quickly realized those things cost money and required time, both of which were in short supply. So the plan was to go on welfare for the first 5 years of his life. That would give me enough time to get a foundation started. I entered into a business school to acquire some skills to secure a job right away. However, in the meantime, I was flipping burgers at a local fast food restaurant. At the time, I wasn't sure what life had in store for me; but I what I did know was I was going to beat the odds.

## *Building the Foundation*

Using some of the skills I got from the school along with my own personal know-how I began my entrepreneurial journey in 1998: "On Point Business Services." I'll never forget it. I created resumes, business cards, typed letters, and other general business services. At the time, I didn't think much of it other than that it was a cool gig that bought in a couple extra bucks while I still worked my regular job. Who would have known that my decision to charge people for my regularly free services would be a life-altering event? On Point was short lived because it wasn't my passion and I grew tired of it. It wasn't fun anymore. I didn't feel energized and fulfilled while I was doing it; however, it did peek my interest as far as working for myself. I just had to find something I enjoyed doing. It took years of trial and error, years of different ventures, years of financial sacrifice and hardship, years of second guessing myself, and wondering if I was kidding myself. After all, when I looked at my friends and family at the time, none of them were entrepreneurs. So why did I think I could step outside the box and do something that no one else around me was doing? I really had no idea. I just knew I needed and desired more than what a 9-5 was giving me. I knew I wanted to be available for my son. I knew I wanted to have the flexibility to create my own schedule. I knew I wanted to be the decider of when I took vacation. I wanted to have the freedom of taking off when I was sick, or taking a personal day without worrying how many days I had already used up. I didn't want to have to schedule my time according to someone else's convenience. And most of all, I wanted complete dominion over when I got paid, how much I got paid, when I got a raise, and what the criteria was for that raise. That was a defining moment that made me realize, traditional 9-to-5 life was not for me. Although I still had to do it for a while to maintain my household, but I knew it wouldn't be forever.

Entrepreneurship is not for the faint of heart. You have to be willing to work hard, work real hard, and then work harder some more. You must be willing to sacrifice physically, emotionally, and financially. You must be willing to serve and give a lot of yourself. You must be willing to learn, to get your feelings hurt, to have thick skin, and not take it personal. Know that theere are going to be good days, and they are going to be bad days. And those bad days may make you want to give up, but you must perservere and keep pushing to produce the results you want.

Many people thought I was crazy the day I decided to finally leave my 9-to-5, that great cushiony job with the security of a check every two weeks. It was scary, I won't lie; but I also knew that anything that was worth doing was going to be scary. Change is scary. Doing something that goes against everything you were brought up to believe is scary. I had to do it. I had to take the chance, because if I didn't I would live with that uncertainty in the back of my mind – woulda, coulda, shoulda. That is a feeling no one should have. Making this decision would either propel me forward or send me back to the workforce. Either way, I felt like I had nothing to lose but everything to gain.

I love being an entrepreneur. It is one of the best decisions I have ever made, and the greatest feeling next to the day I gave birth to my son. I love the fact that I am able to create my own destiny by helping others create theirs. Entrepreneurship brings me a feeling of control, freedom and flexibility. I have a control over what I do and who I work with. I control how much I get paid. I have the freedom to switch gears if and when I want to. I have the flexibility of time and space. Entrepreneurship brings me joy because I get to do what I love and what I was created for on my own terms.

## *Create a Productive Environment*

Today, I am a faith-based empowerment speaker, life and business productivity strategist, and author. I am also known as "The Producer" because my primary function is to help my clients produce the results they want so they can find, embrace, and live in their purpose. My typical clients are new and aspiring speakers, coaches, and authors that need support, accountability, strategies, tools, and resources to get to their next level. Thus far, I've been able to sustain my business and balance my life using the word of God and the same core principles I teach my clients: effective time management, organization, and systems. These methods allow me to work smarter, not harder.

First, it is important for me to priortize and organize my time and my day. It is important to know there are only 1,440 minutes in a given day. So I know I can only fit a certain amount of activities in that time frame. It is also important for me to understand how essential it is for me to get 6 to 8 hours of sleep every night so that I can be productive and coherent the next day. With those things in mind, I jot down all the things I need to accomplish, then the things I want to accomplish for the day. Then using Google Calendar, I assign time frames to all my needs. That includes sleeping, eating, and personal breaks. Yes, "Me Time" breaks are a need in my world to keep me sane. Next, I time the time that I have remaining and I pop it in my wants. If everything doesn't fit then it gets transferred to the next day. That is how I keep my time in check.

Second, I make sure to keep my physical, mental, and even virtual space organized. I always say, "A clean space allows for a clear mind" and that helps me process information effectively, bring forth creativity, and allows me to make informed decisions. So whether it be at home or work, the area I'm in must be neat and organized. I can't concentrate when there is clutter everywhere. I don't know about you, but I start to feel overwhelmed. It's the same way with virtual space. Many people don't realize how confusing and unorganized virtual space can be. This includes all your processing devices i.e. desktops, laptops, cell phones, tablets, etc... It may not be a big deal to the average person, but for entrepreneurs, career professionals, and all around go-getters, this is seemingly unsigificant factor is actually very essential. Having the files in your computer neat and organized is very important. You don't want to waste time because your files are in order. You don't want to waste any precious minutes looking at or scrolling through junk emails. Unsubscribing to those right away eliminate that issue. Setting up categorized file folders in your email is also a helpful strategy to find your emails easily. The last useful tips to staying virtually organized is to make sure that all of your devices are synchronized across the board. So your emails, calendar, contacts, etc., should all be constantly updated and synced throughout the day. This way, regardless of where you are or what device you're using, you will always have the most recent information.

### *Mind Your Thoughts*

Last, let's talk about systems. I believe that there is a system for everything we do in life. Very few people become successful by "winging it". All the people that I look up to as being successful like Oprah

Winfrey, Les Brown, Tony Robbins, Bishop TD Jakes, and Dr. Joyce Meyers, they all speak of the importance of having effective systems to get them through the day. Years ago, I was taught that business systems are composed of three main categories: mindset, strategy, and action. To analyze the system of the mindsets, you'll realize that everything we do and say is a manifestation of something that we've thought. So it is important to have a positive mindset, especially when you're going through a rough patch. We tend to give our negative thoughts so much more power over the positive ones. However, using affirmations are a great way to stay in the positive zone. Starting your statements with words like "I will ...", "I believe ...", and "I can ..." will always put you in a successful frame of mind, to the point where you'll take pride in saying "I did ...." Next, the system of strategy is your planning process. How are you going to accomplish your goals by working smarter not harder? This is where successful leaders use automation. The winning mindset behind successful people is to do the minimum, but control the maximum. So what do I mean by this? Not saying that successful people do not work hard, but they do pick and choose what they work hard at. Meaning, they know how to let go. They focus on their strengths not their weaknesses. They devote the majority of their day to their craft. To do this, focus on automating areas such as appointment scheduling, email and social media marketing, client and prospect follow-ups, etc... The areas that can't be automated, should be delegated. As an effective CEO and leader, your responsibility is not to do everything yourself. Your function is to hire the right people that can perform the back office functions to bring your vision to life, so you can concentrate in your area of expertise. When I first started Find Your Purpose, I couldn't afford to hire employees. I could barely afford to pay myself. However, I knew there were aspects of my business I didn't know how to do, nor did I want to learn. For example, building my website was a need but I didn't have the skills. So I outsourced it to a web designer and just oversaw the process. This freed me up to concentrate on prospecting for new clients, while feeling comfortable knowing that my website was still being constructed. I also outsourced all the graphic work for my flyers and social media. It would have taken me too much time to learn how to do it myself, but don't think I didn't try. I sure did, and I ended up frustrated and extremely overwhelmed. Making the decision to outsource saved me time, money, and aggrevation. Once I released the negative mindset that "I didn't" have the money to pay for the services, I was able to sign new clients to get the money; and ultimately, I was able to be more productive and get more accomplished. The last aspect to effective systems is taking action. This seems pretty simple, but people have the hardest time doing it. All the strategies, processes, and planning will do you no good if you don't implement. Usually when people become stagnant they have to go back to the beginning - their mindset. There's something blocking you from moving forward. For me, it was procrastination stemmed from fear of being rejected due to not having a college degree. Your procrastination point may be different, but the one thing that is the same is until you address it, you will find it hard to be productive. I came to the point where I finally accepted the fact that I was talented and gifted as I was. Eventually I did obtain my degree, which was more to make my mother happy, then it was to progress in my business. Nonetheless, once I changed my mindset, my confidence began to grow and my business began to soar – all because I started to take action.

## *Finding Success in Your Purpose*

Going down the road to success, you have to be flexible, willing to change and adapt.

Athough my son was my original "why" to becoming an entrepreneur, it was 24 years ago. He is a young man now and doesn't require as much of my attention as he did before. So today, I continue this journey of entrepreneurship because I genuinely love what I do. I still love the freedom, flexibility and control. However, now, the thought process surrounding my "why" is more along the lines of building generational wealth and leaving a legacy that my grandchildren's grandchildren can be proud of. I've always had a success and leadership mindset. I didn't recognize it as an adolescent or teenager. I just wanted to get good grades and see things done the proper way. As an adult, I now know that God was preparing me for a time such as this because there are people that need the structure and guidance I possess. I used to think of success from a personal financial and winning standpoint. However, today I know that success is not about my personal gains, but about the positive impact I have on others. Their strides in personal and professional development has become my ultimate success. So I continuously think of different ways to leave my fingerprint on the world. I'm constantly educating myself through reading, podcasts, conferences, mentorship, coaching, networking, etc ... anything I can think of that will elevate my level of thinking and producing, so I can in turn, teach the masses.

Here is what I want you to understand, before I started 'Find Your Purpose,' I had no money. I was barely making ends meet, and I had just lost my house to foreclosure. On the outside, no one could tell the struggles I was going through. I did a pretty good job of keeping that part of my personal life private. Although, I was well known and involved in my community, not many people knew the real story of what I was going through. I had my non-profit that wasn't generating sufficient income, much less turning a profit, but I was making a huge impact on youth and their families. I was feeling good about helping others; meanwhile, I was suffering personally and financially. None of these things were putting food on the table and keeping a roof over my head. I knew something had to change. I couldn't go on the way things were. I knew my strengths but I started to feel worthless. Someone introduced me to the concept of life coaching and getting paid for what they saw as my biggest strength. At the time, I had just finished my run for The Office of New York State Assembly and I had nothing to lose but everything to gain. So I hired a coach to teach me how to become a coach and get certified. That one decision changed the entire course of my life, and after finding my own purpose, I gave birth to "Find Your Purpose." Within a couple of weeks, I got my first client. My confidence was a bit shaky at first because I still didn't fully understanding the value and impact I was making, so I didn't charge my worth. When I did the math, I was making a little more than minimum wage. As my confidence grew, so did my clientele and their progress. That made it easier for me to increase my prices exponentially over time. Fast forward three years, I am well on my way to becoming a six-figure earner, as a full-time entrepreneur. Some days are easier and more excited than others; but either way, I make the best of it by seizing every moment so I can produce the results I want.

# *About Terryl Ebony*

With over 20 years of entrepreneurial experience, combined with her education in human services and community organizing, Terryl Ebony has a wealth of knowledge that transcends her title of Life & Business Productivity Strategist (a.k.a. "The Producer"), faith-based speaker, correspondent, author, and community advocate. As the CEO of Find Your Purpose, Terryl empowers entrepreneurs on national platforms, in groups, and through one on one coaching and consulting. She teaches effective time management, organization, systems, and strategies to help entrepreneurs find, embrace, and live in their purpose, so they can begin producing the results they want.

Terryl was crowned "The Producer" in 2017 when she undoubtedly proved she was the expert at getting the job done. Moving dozens of clients from idea to fruition, from one level to the next, from stuck to action, from procrastination to anticipation, and from working harder to working smarter. Terryl uses an unapologetic - tell it like it is - yet caring and amusing approach of productive strategies to get her message across. She speaks nationally on topics such as: productivity, finding purpose, loving the skin you're in, having a CEO Mindset, creating solid business foundations, etc. Terryl is also a celebrity social media correspondent for conferences and red carpet events. She is also the Founder/Host of the Faith Walk To Purpose Podcast, where she interviews high-income entrepreneurial earners about their faith walk.

# CONCLUSION
*by*
*Marsha Guerrier*

———————————————✳————————————————

This book has been as much a journey for me as it was for you reading it. I am feeling so empowered and have learned so much from these women and I hope you have as well. I'm thankful that these courageous women have opened up about their journeys in order to help guide you through your own experiences as entrepreneurs. Entrepreneurship is not a journey that one should ever take on alone. For the authors, this book was an opportunity to connect and accelerate the mindset of new and aspiring entrepreneurs. I hope and pray that we've done that for you! Surround yourself with people that uplift you and encourage and support your dreams.

My life and journey through entrepreneurship could not have happened if I didn't have the full support of my family. Even my friends that have watched me evolve into a different person supported me enough to lose me to "your new friends" as some of them would say. Part of my strategy along my journey to success was to grow my network of like minded entrepreneurs. I knew in order to maintain the proper mindset I needed to speak this entrepreneur language with those that understand it. Imagine you are learning French and you only speak French to your English speaking friends, what will happen? You will revert back to speaking English and lose all that you've learned in French.

It's the same way in business, having someone to express your disappointments, setbacks, failures and wins with makes a big difference then sharing it with someone whose response won't match that of an entrepreneur. Let's say you have a setback in your business this month's sales did  not go as planned and you share that with a friend that's not in business this is what you may hear "Oh sorry you had a bad month, maybe it's time you focus on work more and put the business on the side." Share that same experience with a colleague in business and here's what you may hear "Oh sorry you had a bad month, so for next month here are a couple of ways I think you can improve your sales strategy to hit your numbers...." See the difference? Your friend, while they mean well will not understand the need to dust your shoulders off and get back at it, while your colleague in business will share with your new ideas and strategies to help you succeed.

After reading this book you have instantly gained a new network of business colleagues that you can call on when you need. The authors have left you their contact details so don't be shy about reaching out to the person that inspired you the most just to say thank you. They are all part of the Women on the Rise Network so join us there  when you're ready to share your story with other women on the Rise! This is  why you purchased this book, it may have been just to support the author but look how much more rewarding it is for you.

They say faith without work is dead. I know you have faith that your business ideas or your ability to make an impact on this earth is real. But it won't come find you; you have to work at your business  and walk in the path that you are destined for. Action follows faith, so what actions are you taking today!

*Marsha Guerrier*

# About Marsha Guerrier

Marsha Guerrier is a bestselling author, speaker, trainer, life balance and business coach, and CEO of Women on the Rise NY, Inc. a small business consulting firm. In addition to being an entrepreneur Marsha also has a full-time career in the financial technology industry spanning over 20 years working for Fortune 500 and startup firms. Marsha is also the founder the Yva Jourdan Foundation a non-profit organization dedicated to helping families with children with special needs and women entrepreneurs and has served as the Executive Director for over 8 years. Marsha holds a BS in Business, Management and Economics. She is a two time recipient of the State Assembly of New York's Women of Distinction Award for both her work with the Yva Jourdan Foundation and Women on the Rise NY, Inc.

Marsha believes that coaching is both a life tool and a business tool. As a strategic, visionary thinker, she has a passion for inspiring people, at all levels, to optimize their full potential while maintaining a focus on goal setting, reflection and life balance. Her book Life Balance for the Women on the Rise gives women the necessary tools to enable them to make significant improvements in five key areas of life. Her clients include Authors, Coaches, Small Business, Non-Profits, and Ministries.

Marsha support women as they learn to organize, prioritize and develop strategies for their personal and professional life. Through Women on the Rise NY, Inc. she provides 1 on 1 and group coaching, a business mastermind group, and an annual Forum & Expo. She is available for panel discussions and workshops on Business Success Startup, Your Business and Your Brand and Using Fear to Motivate You to Succeed.

Website: www.womenontheriseny.com
IG: womenontheriseny
Twitter: @wotrny
Facebook: womenontheriseny
Join our group on Facebook: wearewomenontherise

www.ingramcontent.com/pod-product-compliance
Lightning Source LLC
Chambersburg PA
CBHW071113210326
41519CB00020B/6287